THE BIG BOOK OF COL

AN EDUCATIONAL COUNTRY TRAVEL PICTURE BOOK FOR KIDS ABOUT HISTORY, DESTINATION PLACES, ANIMALS AND MANY MORE

Colombia is a country located in South America.

Which continent does Colombia belong to?

Colombia belongs to South America.

Do Colombians support women to be bosses at workplaces?

Yes, most bosses in workplaces in Colombia are women!

How many oceans does Colombia have coastline on?

Colombia has coastline on the Caribbean Sea and the Pacific Ocean.

What are the people of Colombia called?

The people of Colombia are called Colombians.

When did Colombia get independence?

Colombia got independence on July 20, 1810.

What was the old name of Colombia?

The old name of Colombia was "New Granda".

Where did the name 'Colombia' come from?

Colombia was named after a person, Christopher Columbus.

What is the population of Colombia?

The population of Colombia is over 52.4 million.

How many languages are spoken in Colombia?

There are 37 languages spoken in Colombia.

Are Colombians Hispanic or Latino?

Colombians are Hispanics.

How many species of orchids does Colombia have?

Colombia has 4000 species of orchids!

What is the official name of Colombia?

The official name of Colombia is Republic of Colombia.

Is Colombia a biodiverse country?

Yes, Colombia is known to be the most biodiverse country in the world.

What is the most popular sport in Colombia?

The most popular sport in Colombia is Football.

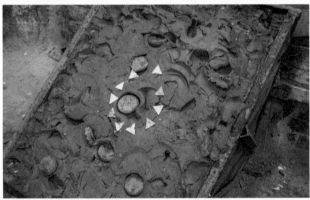

What is the national sport of Colombia?

The national sport of Colombia is called "Tejo".

How many borders does Colombia have?

Colombia has 7 borders.

How often do they play their national anthems?

The government of Colombia has ordered the tv and radio channels to play the national anthem of Colombia two times every day!

Which tree is the national tree of Colombia?

The national tree of Colombia is the wax tree.

What is Colombia known for in terms of exporting goods?

Colombia exports a lot of goods. It is the biggest exporter of deep green emeralds in the world.

Which country does Colombia trade goods with the most?

Colombia trades largely with the US.

Where is the second largest carnival celebrated?

The second largest carnival of the world is celebrated beautifully in Colombia's Caribbean city of Barranquilla.

How many public holidays do they have every year?

Colombians get 18 public holidays every year!

How much of the Amazon rainforest covers Colombia?

About one-third of Colombia is covered by the Amazon rainforest.

How much of Colombia is covered by forests?

About 52% of Colombia is covered by forests.

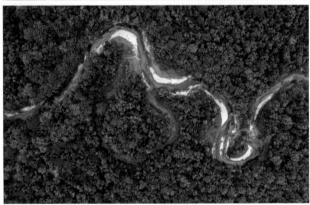

How many active volcanoes are there in Colombia?

There are 6 active volcanoes in Colombia.

How large is Colombia?

Colombia is the 25th largest country in the world.

How big are the palm trees in Colombia?

The palm trees in Colombia are about 200 feet tall!

How many seasons are there in Colombia?

There are only two seasons in Colombia, the dry season and the rainy season.

What is the highest mountain range in Colombia?

The highest mountain range in Colombia is "Sierra Nevada de Santa Marta".

Is Sierra Nevada de Santa Marta considered to be the highest coastal mountain only in Colombia?

No, Sierra Nevada de Santa Marta is the highest coastal mountain of the world.

Is Colombia known to be a happy country?

Yes, Colombians are known to be very happy people.

It is known for its rich biodiversity and is one of the most biologically diverse countries in the world.

The capital city of Colombia is Bogotá. also The largest city in Colombia is Bogotá.

The official language spoken in Colombia is Spanish.

Colombia is the only country in South America with coastlines on both the Pacific Ocean and the Caribbean Sea.

The country is famous for its coffee production. Colombian coffee is renowned worldwide for its quality.

Colombia is home to several indigenous tribes, each with its own unique culture and traditions.

The national dance of Colombia is called cumbia, which is a vibrant and energetic dance style.

The Andes Mountains run through Colombia, offering breathtaking landscapes and opportunities for hiking and trekking.

Colombia is home to many colorful and diverse bird species, including toucans and hummingbirds.

The country has a variety of climates, ranging from tropical rainforests to snowy mountains.

Colombia has a rich history of gold mining, and gold artifacts can be found in museums across the country.

The Colombian flag consists of three horizontal stripes: yellow, blue, and red.

Colombia is known for its vibrant and colorful festivals, such as the Carnaval de Barranquilla and the Feria de Cali.

Colombia is a country that offers diverse landscapes, friendly people, and a rich cultural heritage, making it an exciting destination for tourists to explore.

The country has numerous national parks and natural reserves, offering opportunities for eco-tourism and wildlife spotting.

Colombia is the second-largest producer of emeralds in the world.

The currency used in Colombia is called the Colombian peso.
The Colombian currency has various denominations, including coins of 50,
100, 200, 500, and 1,000 pesos, and bills of 1,000, 2,000, 5,000, 10,000,
20,000, 50,000, and 100,000 pesos.

The salt cathedral of Zipaquirá is an underground church built within a salt mine and is a popular tourist attraction.

Colombia has a diverse cuisine, with dishes like arepas (corn cakes) and bandeja paisa (a traditional platter of beans, rice, meat, and more).

The official Colombian dance is called the salsa, and you can find salsa clubs in many cities.

The Amazon River, one of the longest rivers in the world, begins its journey in Colombia.

Colombia has several beautiful beaches, including the beaches of Tayrona National Park and San Andrés Island.

Colombia is home to unique wildlife, such as the colorful poison dart frogs and the giant anteater.

The Colombian people are known for their warmth and friendliness towards visitors.

In which colours does the Canó Cristales change?

It uniquely changes its colour between red, blue, black, yellow, and green.

Is Colombia home to unique animals?

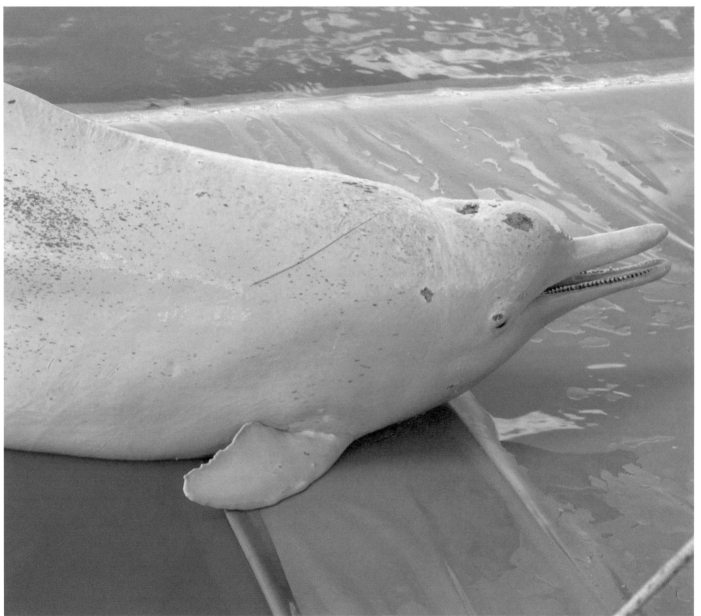

Yes, Colombia is a home to many unique animals. One of which is a pink dolphin!

Which river is the most unique in Colombia?

"Cano Cristales" also known as the River of Five Colours is in Colombia!

When does the river change its colour?

The river changes its colour between September and November.

The country has a vibrant street art scene, with colorful murals and graffiti adorning many city walls.

Colombia is the world's leading producer of flowers, especially roses.

The pre-Columbian city of Ciudad Perdida, also known as the Lost City, is an ancient archaeological site hidden deep in the jungle.

The country is named after Christopher Columbus, the explorer who arrived in the Americas in 1492.

The Quindío wax palm is the national tree of Colombia and can grow up to 60 meters tall.

The Colombian carnival of Blacks and Whites in Pasto is recognized as a UNESCO Intangible Cultural Heritage.

Colombia is home to El Cocuy National Park, which features majestic snow-capped mountains.

The Colombian city of Medellín is known for its innovative urban transportation system, including cable cars and escalators in hilly areas.

Colombia has seven UNESCO World Heritage Sites, including the historic center of Santa Cruz de Mompox and the Coffee Cultural Landscape.

The Colombian peso symbol is $, just like the US dollar, but the currency names are different.

Colombia's national flower is the orchid, which is one of the largest flower families in the world.

The Colombian Caribbean coast is famous for its white sand beaches and crystal-clear waters.

Colombia has a variety of traditional musical styles, including vallenato, cumbia, and bullerengue.

Colombia is the second-most biodiverse country in the world, after Brazil.

The San Agustín Archaeological Park in Colombia features impressive stone statues created by an ancient civilization.

Colombia is home to a unique natural phenomenon known as the Caño Cristales, or the "Liquid Rainbow," a river with vibrant colors during certain times of the year.

TOP 10 TRAVEL TIPS FOR VISITING COLOMBIA

1. Safety: Like any other destination, it's important to take precautions while traveling in Colombia. Stay informed about the current safety situation in the areas you plan to visit and follow the advice of local authorities and your tour guide.

2. Climate and Packing: Colombia has diverse climates, so pack accordingly. Bring lightweight and breathable clothing for warmer regions, and warmer clothes for higher elevations. Don't forget sunscreen, a hat, and insect repellent.

3. Learn Basic Spanish: While it's possible to get by with English in major cities and tourist areas, learning a few basic Spanish phrases can greatly enhance your travel experience and help you communicate with locals.

4. Money Matters: Carry both cash and cards. In larger cities and tourist areas, credit cards are widely accepted, but have some local currency (Colombian pesos) on hand for smaller establishments or rural areas where cards may not be accepted.

5. Transportation: Colombia has a well-developed transportation network. Domestic flights are convenient for longer distances, and buses are a popular option for traveling within the country. Use reputable transportation companies and be cautious with your belongings.

6. Try Local Cuisine: Colombia offers a variety of delicious dishes. Don't miss out on trying traditional foods like arepas, empanadas, bandeja paisa, and fresh tropical fruits. Be cautious when consuming street food and drink bottled water to stay hydrated.

7. Explore Coffee Culture: Colombia is famous for its coffee. Consider visiting a coffee plantation to learn about the coffee-making process and taste some of the finest coffee in the world.

8. Respect Local Customs: Colombians are known for their warmth and friendliness. Show respect for local customs and traditions, such as greeting people with a handshake or a hug, and being mindful of dress codes when visiting religious sites.

9. Stay Hydrated: Colombia's climate can be hot and humid, especially in coastal areas. Drink plenty of water to stay hydrated and avoid heat-related illnesses. Be cautious with tap water and opt for bottled water or use a water purifier.

10. Embrace the Culture: Colombia has a rich cultural heritage. Immerse yourself in the vibrant music, dance, and festivals that the country has to offer. Engage with locals, learn about their traditions, and be open to new experiences.

Made in United States
Troutdale, OR
12/19/2024

27007109R00026